The Profane Earth

The Profane Earth

By Ollivier Dyens

Mansfield Press

Copyright © Ollivier Dyens 2004
All Rights Reserved
Printed in Canada

Library and Archives Canada Cataloguing in Publication

Dyens, Ollivier
   The profane earth / Ollivier Dyens.

Poems.
Translation, by the author, of excerpts of Les bêtes and
   Les murs des planètes.
ISBN 1-894469-17-8

   I. Title.

PS8557.Y45P76 2004   C841'.54   C2004-906292-1

Cover Design: Ollivier Dyens
Interior Design: Marijke Friesen

Mansfield Press wishes to thank VLB Éditeur for permission to translate
from *Les Murs des planètes suivi de La cathédrale aveugle* and Éditions
Triptyque for permission to translate from *Les Bêtes*.

The publication of *The Profane Earth*
has been generously supported by
The Canada Council for the Arts and
The Ontario Arts Council.

Mansfield Press Inc.
25 Mansfield Avenue, Toronto, Ontario, Canada M6J 2A9
Publisher: Denis De Klerck
www.mansfieldpress.net

To Sonja,
to Shane,

to Bruce Cockburn
whose songs have moved me tremendously throughout the years,

and my heartfelt thanks to Denis and Nuria.

Between the wish and the thing the world lies waiting.
—Cormac McCarthy

Recreating Poetry

Poetry is like a fractal: infinite in space, outside of time, both disorderly and symmetrical. In the poetic realm, turbulences create salient forms, rare emotions; words, images, rhythm fusing into an ephemeral, almost invisible glow penetrating one's heart. A poem, by nature, is elusive and cannot be held or restrained. A translator, then, never dissects, never dissembles but rather folds and unfolds, each time moving closer to the poem's essence.

The poems you are about to read were originally published in French in two different books called *Les Murs des planètes* and *Les Bêtes*. When Denis De Klerck, the publisher of Mansfield Press, first offered me the chance to publish these poems in English, I suggested that he let me tackle the translation. This in spite of the fact that I do not consider myself a translator for I know how difficult the task is and I also know how much talent is needed to initiate such a task. A good translator is as rare as a good writer, for both engage in creating sense out of the world's disarray and confusion; both try to create symmetry out of society's transient, skilfully cruel nature. So why translate my own poetry then? For the boundless new possibilities that the English language offers, for the delight of seeing my poems twice born, for the wonder of having to explore a territory and transforming myself as I do so, and for the danger implicit in such an exploration. I came into this English translation carrying images, metaphors and sounds that were particular to my perception of French. Would I be able to let go of my original words, to free my initial emotions and let them mature in another language? Or would I simply lose my way and wander, deaf and mute, into English's particular dominion? What a wonderfully frightening question to ask oneself.

My original creative process, in French, implies the generating, in my mind, of a tableau whose colours, sounds and emotions I strive (and frequently struggle) to decipher and render into language. This rendering, in my most abstract poems, often exceeds words and emerges as more texture than story. I could not, therefore, translate some of my poems, for their original French version was drawing on language in such a particular way, creating such convoluted textures, that no amount of translating would do. My only option was to reconstruct the initial creative process using the original French poems as the imaginative tableaux. From there, I could extract a specific texture from each French tableau and sow it into English, hoping it would gather strength from this new emotional universe. But to do that, I had to abandon the text and concentrate on the visual, emotional and rhythmic quality of the poem. Thus, the poems you will read, especially in the book's first part, are not translations as much as they are recreations.

Here then are my poems. I hope that at least one may become a small island from which the shores of this extraordinary world we live in can be seen.

Ollivier Dyens
September 2004

One

-I-

Here is
my love
covered with moths
burning quietly
in years of disquiet
whispering in my mouth
like a psalm of nails
her breast
as young as water
her hand
like a river of absence
between my thighs
her eyes
shuddering
like rare animals
in blooms
of silence.

-2-

An oriole collapses
in your chest
withering
slowly
in its own echo
filling our closeness
with a sound
like that of the oboe
All I can see
now
is this light
carrying the rhyme
of origins
this light
out of which
nothing
ever arises
but
the shape
of darkness.

-3-

Turn your head and
look at me
covered with the rustling
of thistle
pissing on flowers
as if they were
God's fingers

In the strange marrow of centuries
you undress
dreaming
of calves and heifers
of dogs
forever
walking
in empty rooms
lapping
orifices
breathing
lazily
dogs
barking like men
bent
in torrents of coal.

-4-

In the reign of voices
whispers
the meander of pain
yells
the child
naked in braille
devoured
by hail
In the reign of voices
ravens hunger
so quietly
in my throat
that nothing
not even your tongue
can heal me
from the weight of stones

Silence
pungent of pungent rivers
like an exile of bones
your hands are bread
your face
untamed in my skull
is an endless rain of insects
that hatch
in a veil of willows.

-5-

Rule over me
eel in my bed
slithering in wounds
(your eyes are the colour of lilies, much heavier than the ocean)
a thousand cocoons
in your mouth
like semen on a tree

hooves on my soles, my forehead swollen, my tongue distended, the
stench, the noise, the warmth of lilacs, the sky again and again,
curved like fingers, on a neck, on a breast, fingers

the calf sheathed
with metal
and misery
the shelamb
staring at my mother
mating with the tree trunk

my head in the rain, the toads hiding in my kidneys
deflowering
the water
in failure
I yell out your name
but hear nothing
neither clouds nor gods

You are the violent tree
in my ailing father
the twisted
and unspeakable
hurt
that walls my face.

-6-

My love
carved
in my nails, in my arms
on my legs
like a crow
beneath my eyes
my love
like bark
piercing my skull
weeds unfolding
in my lungs
my love
braided with limbs
circled
with thirst
my love
like a hundred thousand
preys
swirling in the distance.

-7-

Heal me
tarred with memory
and decay
unspoken
in your chalice of flesh
Heal me
again
so often and
forever gently
while a young girl
laced with islands and scales
fastens herself to me, her feet smaller
than your eyes, her nape
warm as milk, her scent
as deep
as the fir tree

Barley undulates
like a soft floating
womb
We fall asleep
entangled
dreaming of each other
lost in forests of giant mangroves
lush with salt
and atonement.

-8-

Wallowing in your liver
I urinate in pools of blood, swallow fields of gullet,
quench my thirst with scared vulva
Wallowing in your liver
my nuzzle in the fever of turtles, my teeth in shredded bowels
I bark
three hundred times
as everything wakes up, hunts, kills and runs away

But under the covenant of cedars
hyenas ejaculate
and geese settle down

Now in the languor of burden
horses are prowling
like gestures on grass
and the sky opens through me
with faint thunder.

-9-

Embrace me
moaning animal
lewd with rupture
quavering
against my teeth
plunder me with light
sow my jaw with mud
and tear my lips away
your sex on my palate
like a talisman of flesh
a wet octopus
in your thighs

your tongue fills out my mouth
with salt
with hair
with the blackness of birth
and your hand sinks into my hand
with semen
and
swaying.

-10-

You press on my eyes
with prowling
fingers
lay my lips
on the lamb's teat
my loins
on lakes
of asylum
your hands breaking bread
offering sorrow
to the wandering world

Look at me
clawing
at your name
fasten to your stomach
bowed
forever
to you
until pain
becomes
a hyacinth
of dusk.

-II-

In yields of revelation
you wake next to me
young suddenly
against my legs
covering my eyes
with moss and rain
your breasts
like an altar of chalk
soft with the age
of so many
hands
a flower
of milk
arched in marble

do not speak, do not speak
rest in yearning
those are the years
of despair
the bones
of communion
do not speak
for I know
you
for you
are
here
bequeathed in grace
lying in bed
covered with brine
your tongue
like an abbey of longing
pressing
against my eyes

There is no want for hope
no wish

for deliverance
our love
is a forest
of quiescence
where
the frightened fawn
heaves
where roes run
nervously
where mules
suckle
forever
where eyeless morays
quiver in your breasts
and foxes
bore into me
where the ebb of grass
presses lightly
on the symmetry of petals

do not look at me
turn around
fall back to sleep
the line of your back
warm against my chest
your hand resting
on the pillow
like a broken iris
calling me to this place
between our love
where God kneels
in obscurity
unable
to name the world
to ease the fear
unable
to touch His face
to pull out
His eyes.

-12-

You're mating
in my
throat
vast
and diseased
snails
on my tongue sperm
on your breast
pus on the tallith
Mary of shame
of malice
and surrender.

-13-

When I raise my eyes
all I see
is her
unbearable
beneath a refuge
of filth and lovers
When I raise my eyes
all I see
is the linen of her breath
and the edges of the sun
in the chorale
of her spirit
the water lilies
of her words
folding over my hands
like slow seaweed

When I raise my eyes
all I see
is her name
in my palms
like a garden of salt
her shoulders
like mares at dawn
When I raise my eyes
all I see
is her
lying in bed
her breasts
moist with light
deep in the ewe's mouth
her thighs
like birds of lust
adrift
in thunder.

Two

-14-

The world is made
whole
with everything that dies
in the peaceful
indifference
of the spirit
The world is made
whole
with everything that loves
ceaselessly
desperately
leaving
faint traces
a displaced pebble
a wounded animal
a wind
lingering on someone's lips
the waning sigh
of a newborn
pierced by psalms
and kingdoms

We are neither dust
nor ashes
blood nor flesh
only memories
wandering
the ocean of centuries
neither the heavens
stars nor salt
are as deep as
the taste of berries
in my throat
neither creation nor its wonders
are enough
to hold on to you
nothing can help me

drink the marsh's hymen
nothing can help me
injure myself
in you

~

One day in Louisiana
we took the car
and drove aimlessly
but after a few hours
we found
a road which led
to the Gulf of Mexico

On the side of this road
perfectly maintained
where no signs had been posted
we saw
a cemetery
at the foot of some trees
It was late
we stopped
shadows
swelling in the branches
tumbling
between us
like the fragrance of time
in a horizon
crippled with birds

We walked
between three oak trees
among the coffins
lying
in no particular order
above the ground
Only one
had a name
a fragile violet
in the rain

small enough for an infant
The others were mute
worn by memory

And everywhere
the silence of innocence
of maggots
the silence of stillness
of dandelions
the silence
of everything that suffocates
and knows
its soul
is but a murmur
in the black prayers
of men
and beasts

∻

Even in death
one can be abandoned
and even rocks
that sentence us
to the earth's mire
can be forgotten
Some die alone
and are buried
in a coffin
at the foot of a tree
at the side of a road
where harmless tourists
stunned
by so much loneliness
stop
and stare
but remain blind
until the twilight
has darkened.

-15-

When Sonja falls asleep
I find myself alone
in the living room
watching television
and feeling the weight of the house
around me
Sometimes
I turn off
the volume
and eavesdrop on the song
of locusts
I want to get up
and hide among them
forget everything
but their ancient
rustle of hymns
and only be aware
of their rare
and everlasting
horizon

but I lay still
my head resting awkwardly
on worn pillows
looking at endless shows
endlessly saying nothing
the hours
besiege me
harbour of chasms
filled with emptiness

Every evening
I abide
while Sonja sleeps
lying in a cage so sharp
its walls are never seen
my eyes drained

in the slough of machines
that never know
never stop

Eventually I get up
open the bedroom door
and witness
my wife
in the foliage
of night
a child
asleep
on the warm sand
of peace
her chest goes up and down
like a wave
dreaming
of being found

Outside
the locusts are still singing
on an auburn hillock
a squirrel swiftly
pauses
Slowly
carefully
I pull the sheets
they smell
of movements and words
and lie down
next to you
Everything's quiet now
abandoned
by what's strong enough
to live
and survive.

-16-

I know this town
where
in the evening
waves of birds
swell in the air
flying, diving, tumbling
above the main street
ripples of millennia
in an arabesque of hills
and rebirth

∽

Everything that breathes
is but a trace
in a dream
a worm
burrowing
through darkness
everything that hurts
is only a resonance
the rustling
of spring
under ice
a shrew
shivering
in smouldering
grass
the eyes of an insect
as nameless as dawn

Life has no purpose
no direction
its oaths are
bare temples
forever calling
to a blindness
Everything exists

just to exist
all that we love
and destroy
all that we injure
and forsake
is a frail forgery
in the boundless flow
of hunger
and remembrance

∵

I lay my hand into yours
and point to the sky
above us
birds of dust
scattered by the age
stare back at us
but you do not
speak
nor stop
nor look at me
I grab your arm
and hold on to you
forcing you to listen
to a thousand estuaries
howling
in the equator of origin.

-17-

The world is filled with splendour
a butterfly
bewildered
fluttering
in the cat's mouth
a loon
woven with shards
and eons
twirling
in the mind
forever drunk
with the prowl of sorrow

The world is filled with splendour
the first collapse
within you
which uncoils
to forever
disappear
never to be
again
like heat
in the grassland
which can only be seen
from a distance
splinter of eyes
bowels
flesh

The world is filled with splendour
and magnificence
nurtured
in manure
cleansed in suffering
beauty
born

of filth
and insects

∶∼

When I get close to you
my shadow
always
precedes me
Before my end
we will stray
together
like burning hawks
in the coral
of sunrise.

-18-

To everyone
living in this city
of streets and winds
called Montreal
let me tell you
of this world
where my wife
held me
not once but twice
at seven
and then
at twenty-five
The first time in winter
in a working class school
on Jean-Talon street
the walls reeking with sweat
and the smell of hot dogs
two trees bounded with asphalt
in the schoolyard
where
one day
I picked up a caterpillar
and brought it back home with me
only to understand
finding it dead
a few hours later
that life must pant
to witness
light
And the second time
at my sister's house
this face so familiar
drawn in me
like secret shivers
eighteen years earlier
these eyes
like haze

unravelling quietly
so not to disturb
the dreaming leaves
To everyone
living in Montreal
let me tell you
how much I miss my home
my city
how much I despise her
and can't stop thinking
of her

A city is a scent
a series of sidewalks
clouds of dirt
rising from speeding trucks
the sound of a key
opening a door
A city is a bus
closing in
finally
in January
a dog
dreaming of brightness
its head resting on a pillow
a soft radio
in a taxi
skidding
on the snowy road
slowly going through
a red light
a stranger
whose eyes I can't see
whose life
might be emptied
of love
and history

∼

The sun
slides
across the table
reaches my hands
warms
the bedroom
pregnant with echoes
and traces
of your body
barely out the house now
walking gingerly
in the foul
soiled snow
and the need to breathe
soars into me
and the cat wakes
in the middle of
our creation
lying on the wooden floor
drunk with heat
and alive
on this earth.

-19-

I was quite sick
that day
my heart thrashing in my chest
my head
like a forest of pain
filled with
the tentacles of unknown animals
listening to the noise
of the world
through my walls
the fever
of all things
washing over me
a restless hive of snakes
stranding me on an ageless
continent
beyond confines
and language

In the middle of the night
I woke up and realized
that my white cat
had jumped on the bed
sat tenderly on my chest
and had begun to purr
I raised my head
and looked
at him
my seventeen years
blind and beautiful
companion
I was terrified
of losing
but lost anyway
a few months later
at a vet
whose clinic

facing the highway
was filled with cages
of demise
and loss
clean as anything
that has surrendered
That's where my cat died
that's where his warmth
his eyes
his grace
vanished
all the years
we lived within each other's slow journey
and grew into each other's movements
dissolving
simply
like smoke from a cigarette

I lowered my head
laid my hand on his back
and felt his limbs stretching fully
his eyes barely open

Far above us
in the cold lagoon
of endlessness
stars shimmered
in dark matter
colossal fires
singing silently
through eternity.

-20-

We always had cats in our house
often two sometimes even three
and over the years
I came to understand them
comfort them
and they
in turn
learned how to delight me
glide secretly
beautifully
next to me at night
as mysterious as fragrance
that traces vision
these cats spread all over my pillows and clothes
strange creatures
born in splendour
and ravishment

Season after season
I saw these peaceful animals
grow older, slower
serene
but I
gorged with embers
could never accept
that life is a fountain
that forever
withers
that only larvae
swallow the scars
that there is
one necessity
not to live
but to exist

~

One day this orange cat—
I had found
on the street
in winter
ten years earlier
and had to tame
slowly
and could only touch
gently
for an animal
like a man
or a woman
can forever consent
to solitude—
jumped on my knees
as he would often do
expecting to coil up next to me
but because
surprisingly
he stank of urine
I pushed him away
and instead of leaping over my hand
he fell to the floor
so sick he could hardly stand up
I hadn't seen it coming
I hadn't noticed anything
it's the truth
I have stopped
lying
I brought him to the vet
who lowered his eyes
and said
"you can leave
if this is too difficult for you"
and like a coward
that's what I did

∻

Abandon me
with all

I ever held
ever kissed
my head buried
in the radiance of fear
Abandon me
for no reason
for I deserve none
for I deserve nothing
neither the day that rises
nor the maggots
neither the sidewalks nor the sky
neither sparrows nor the spider-covered lily
Abandon me
neither loved
nor forgiven
unseen and forgotten
suffocating
quietly
in prairies of wounds
and disgrace.

-21-

My mother and I were sitting
in a downtown restaurant
somewhere west of McGill
I was thirteen
and today this image
of my mother facing me
her bag
hanging from the chair
sitting
in this place
built of neon
and paper towels
is the first thing
that remains
The other
is confusion
my sister has left the house
she's fifteen
my father is away
the bathroom door is open
half finished plates
lie
on a counter
a few men
some women
mumble
continuously
alone
and alone
everything's crumbling, dangling, sticking
like a grove of thistle

But I'm hungry
it's the only thing
I can think about
I'm hungry
my mother is here

in her world that whirls
and lacerates
but I'm hungry
and mom to comfort me
orders my favourite dish
a club sandwich
like we used to get
all of us
after our Sunday swim at the Y
my sister and I sitting
together
facing our parents

The waiter brings the club sandwich
and my mother begins
she tells me things
so painful
they rupture
the membrane
of movements
she needs to say those things
for no one is listening
but me
But I go on eating
I want to stop
but I can't
and everything sickens me
my hands on the toasted bread
my feet
cold and damp
my eyes
unable to look at her
my hair my legs my stomach
everything sickens me
but I go on eating

∼

When living
things
harm each other

nothing in this universe
of brilliance
reacts
nor cares
and
the sorrow of a soul
or the agony of a dog
is but emptiness
at the foot of a shooting star
closing in on the sun
But for us
the world can only be set
ablaze
in the pale light
of entangled flesh
and the immeasurable
exists only
in the realm
of yearning

There are so many moments
we regret
but can't take back
and are forced to live with
so many words
so much disarray
cowardice
we must
wake with and dream with
forever walk with
all this despair
which shapes us
and forces us
to confront
what we seed
ugliness
grief
failure
all these things
suckling at our heart

while we sit here
hands on knees
head bowed
faced with the burden
of being
and with the reach
of defeat
alive in
this life
that
never
yields.

-22-

We had gone to Tunisia
to visit my father's country
I was only five
but I remember
the sand
like hemispheres of pearl
glowing against the sole
of my sandals

Two things
are etched in my mind
The first is the man selling chameleons
that would stick
to your arm
like slivers of age
these motionless
alien animals
for whom life
is a slow tapestry of light
in folds of time
The second is
the travelling florist
selling bouquets
of jasmine
so sweet it made me light-headed

White as childbirth
immense
as fear
jasmine
is a sanctuary
an exile
death
running through a man's hands
the lightness of hay
on a child's tomb
the leather sweetness of dates and figs

sheets
damp from the wind
brushing against the shutters

:~

So many things
live outside
our world
outside our
loneliness
and exist within their own
torment
So many things
bond to the slow breath
of eternity
ignore us
deliberately
deaf
to our bewilderment
A snake
on a wall of lime
a rock
falling in the valley
a laurel tree
crashing
on a litter of mice
a bee
trembling in the alveolus

Always
we are
defeated
forever betrayed
by what's been granted to us
broken up
by fields of poppies
swaying in light
crippled
by the fiery glory
of the praying mantis

copulating
in the emerald of day

Always
we walk away
stroking
our genitals
shielding our eyes
swallowing ashes
seeking
ramparts
roofs
windows
and pretending
to be alive

There is
nothing
no house
no home
no land
for the world
forever
escapes
for the desert
forever
grows
and the eagle crashes into the wall
All is imprint
And the jasmine is fading
And the lizard is sleeping
tiny islands
in the twilight.

-23-

Lift up my eyes to the hills
My dad would say
Where does my help come from?
My help comes from the Lord
The Maker of heaven and earth
He will not let your foot slip
He who watches over you will not slumber
Indeed, He who watches over Israel will neither slumber nor sleep
The Lord watches over you
He is your shade at your right hand
The sun will not harm you by day nor the moon by night
The Lord will keep you from all harm
He will watch over your life
The Lord watches over your coming and going
Both now and forevermore

and a grace
would linger and wane
in the bends of my father's voice
in the hems
of my mother's hands

∻

We were driving
in winter
at night
mom was at home
Isabelle was sitting in front
next to dad
We had come to the top of Côte-des-Neiges
from where
a great part of the city is visible
something
like a shin
that skilfully
fractures
in a flood of steel

The radio was on
Isabelle and dad
were talking
over the wipers continuous
grinding
I don't remember
what was said
but suddenly Isabelle raised her voice
and dad answered
"I hope it kills me"

Outside
the rain
had become
a chapel of thorns
defacing
everything
my father my sister
walls
sidewalks
streets
reaching to my mother
waiting at home
in her rage

I was seven
Days, weeks
even hours
seemed to live
outside the bound of illusion
so infinite
were they
I started to cry
I didn't want to wander
forever
seeking
my father's name
forever
waiting
for something

a flicker
a shade of memory
something that would
shatter my jaw
and puncture my palate
something
like light
lying in darkness

But gradually
I calmed down
Isabelle and dad
had stopped talking

~

Lift up my eyes to the hills
my dad would say
but there are no hills
and shade
revels in death
the sun harms during the day
the moon hurts at night
no one
keeps watch
no one
is there
ever
when we let go
when
we
capitulate.

-24-

Everyday
we fail
under the morning glare
like mindless crabs
knocked against the pebbles
All is violent
and sometimes
life rises
but so briefly
that the child wakes up
and pushes his mother's arm
away
that bread
is fouled by blood
that bereaved and simple
trees
tender their blossoms
like a church of dusk

We rule over the mosaic
of all that is frightened
and feels in its brain
the perpetuity of the sun
the light which springs forth
on a naked breast
over a tongue
kissing a corpse
above a finger
puncturing
an anus
We rule
in the splinters
of lies
in the slaughterhouse
of order
in days
of bawling animals

in brittle trees
of shame
We rule
over everything
like juvenile
gods
pissing away
their misery

∴

One day I saw
a heron
a few feet from me
on the side of the road
reeling
under the storm
his eyes like lead
his left wing
broken
against his side

I got closer
but he drew back and fell even more deeply
in the ditch
I held out my hand
and saw the wind
holler
in his head
I stopped
and looked at him
he looked back
both of us caught
in a place
unsullied
by clemency
a world
where stones
dream of pain

∴

Nations and continents
are never very different
the men you meet
the women you embrace
are always
somehow
alike
living in rooms
where no one knows how to
truly love
The market fruits are the same colour
and burst under the same teeth
the same hand touches the skirt
brushes against the thigh
and rises to the same desire
and the same boy
barely listens to the barking dog
to the braking car
to the woman turning off her radio
and thinking
of nothing

∵

In the language of darkness
the heron collapses peacefully
broken up by the wind
I raise my head
and think of you
to stop me
from hearing.

-25-

It was early morning
in July
I stirred slowly
exhausted from the overwhelming heat
of Montreal
so large, so obese
weariness
is its only anchor
A howl, a moan
something
awakened me
I couldn't tell what
dreams were still decaying
over me
my muscles sore
from sleeping too much
in this apartment
I rented from my father

Outside
the noise came clearly
now
a dog was barking
but that didn't surprise me for the same dog barked
every morning
a husky
which belonged to our neighbours
A stunning dog
his side, his jaw, his claws
made of blood and desire
abused, neglected
confined to a few feet on the balcony
from which
of course
he could never leave

∵

How many dogs have I seen since?
tied to a leash
to a tree
maybe the rope is flexible
and maybe the dog can run
a few feet to the left
and maybe there is a small doghouse
in which he can lie
under a taut and vicious rain
but always he is tied up
unable to see
that the lawn is filthy
that a hive has formed
under the gutter
that a hand brushes against a face
that a small girl
has fallen on the stairs
that lovers wrong each other
in the disease
of humankind
that everything everywhere is calling
screaming bawling
How many dogs have I seen since?
strangled by their leash
howling
for time to stop
for someone's hand
to bring them in
to touch their stomach
and fill them with warmth and dignity

∾

I didn't know what to do
so I went out
on the balcony
which had a view on my father's garden
the one he had created
planting and growing eclipses in it
and I saw the dog barking at a cat
a tiny cat

frightened to death
caught
on top of the fence
a few feet
one or two
from the dog

I got a broom and tried to pull him to our side
but was only able to throw him off balance
The cat
shitting himself
grabbed the fence with all his strength
his fear like treason
greater
than beauty

So I stopped
Around us
buildings were glowing under the morning light
and one after the other
streets emerged from night
a creation
made of waste
and pigeons

After a while
I went back to bed
leaving the cat
and the dog
within their world

I fell asleep eventually
hiding
in apathy
like I always do
and when I woke up a little later
everything was quiet

I never saw the cat again
but for a long time
that dog lived next to me

∴

We believe that God talks to us
through His sacred texts
that He listens when we pray
We believe that God
shines
in the miracle of nature
that He recognizes us and understands
what we are
we believe that God is here
somewhere
in the hollowness
that embroiders the planet
that He trembles
when the lips of a man
taste a woman's breast

But God is a dog
a donkey
a rat
giving us birth
in the immensity of the void
He is the dregs
the foam
the tongue
that penetrates the mouth

Tirelessly
we deny
turning our head
walking away
from the spirit
holding
a flowerless path
in our hands
one

we must take
our legs broken
our teeth shattered
encircled
by nails
lost
in coincidence.

-26-

We lived
on top of a hill
from where the bay
would draw everyone's gaze
facing a horizon so vast
it would defile
the depth of emptiness
and give the impression
of nesting in a forgotten
painting

On the road
next to our house
our cat was killed
barely a month
after our arrival
I had called out his name
again and again
only to find him
in the morning
dead
on the side of the road
as if someone had laid him
gently
his tongue sticking out
his eyes still open
but hard
and cold
a thin layer of skin
covering the bottom part
of his pupil
his black coat
as beautiful and silky
as it ever was

I found a shovel
and buried him

Later
in the afternoon
I came to believe
that the cat wasn't dead
but just unconscious
from the cold
and was now buried
alive
I ran
and dug him up
went straight back to the house
and then
for a long time
used the hair dryer
on this rigid and icy
body
I used to know

A year later
a scrawny fir tree
that never really
matured
was covering
the hole
It was morning
Sonja was fixing up the earth around it
when she stopped
suddenly
I was on the terrace
and called to her
but she didn't answer
I thought she was looking at a mouse
at an object
at something
I drew closer
and she looked at me
in her hands
I saw a bone
a small
collarbone

I stopped
and Sonja lowered her head
her eyes soiled with stones
we were still
unable to move
Behind us
we could hear the wind
whirling forever
in the flesh
of wheat.

Ollivier Dyens is Associate Professor at Concordia University in Montreal. He is the author of numerous books, including *Les Murs des planètes suivi de La cathédrale aveugle* (VLB Éditeur), short listed for the Prix de poésie Terrasses Saint-Sulpice de la revue Estuaire, *Continent X, Vertige du Nouvel Occident* (VLB Éditeur), long listed for the Prix Roberval, *Metal and Flesh, The Evolution of Man, Technology Takes Over* (MIT Press) whose French version was awarded Best Essay from La Société des écrivains canadiens, *Les Bêtes* (Éditions Triptyque), and *Navigations technologiques* (VLB Éditeur).